T0065534

GOD'S TIMETABLE ACCORDING TO THE 7 FEASTS OF ISRAEL

BARBARA WEHMAN

authorHOUSE®

AuthorHouse™
1663 Liberty Drive
Bloomington, IN 47403
www.authorhouse.com
Phone: 833-262-8899

Published by AuthorHouse 03/08/2021

ISBN: 978-1-6655-0456-0 (sc)
ISBN: 978-1-6655-0455-3 (e)

Print information available on the last page.

Contents

Acknowledgments

First, all thanks and praise to my loving and patient heavenly Father, who prodded me gently along about writing this book when I didn't really want to.

I pray You will be glorified by it, and I pray that people who read it will become more aware and amazed about how You have been working out Your plan throughout the ages.

Secondly, I thank my daughter Sara for her help in getting this book published. She has the computer skills which I lack, as well as better eyesight than I have. Were it not for her patient and willing help and encouragement, this book would be at a standstill!

Thank you so much, Sara (Sally), I love you with all my heart!

Prologue

In the beginning…

In the beginning was God…

In the beginning was love…

There was always love, because there was always God.

In the beginning was the Holy Trinity…

There has always been love – passionate love among the three Persons of the Godhead – Father, Son, and Holy Spirit.

There is nothing love wants more than to confer that love on someone else.

God is also a God of order. The universe – the multitude of galaxies – does not fly off into space. God has set them in orbits – gravitational pull.

So, we might say that God is a God of order, and that order is love; God is a God of love and that love is order.

So God began to create. First He created the angelic host. We don't know how long ago in eternity past they were created, but a point came when a third of them rebelled. They were led by Lucifer, where he is referred to in Isaiah 14 and Ezekiel 28.

Revelation 5:11 says there are ten thousand times ten thousand, and thousands of thousands of angels.

The story of the devil's (or Lucifer's) fall is told in Revelation 12.

God fervently loved the angels; He still loves those who stayed true to Him. But they cannot procreate.

At some point in eternity, God decided to create beings that were made in His image. He wanted to make them with a free will to *choose* to love Him and obey Him.

Love can only be satisfied when it is given without compulsion.

So He first made a man, then out of man's side He made a woman, Genesis 2:7-9, 18-25.

God created man (and woman) to love, and who of their own free will would love him back.

Man and woman were created to love each other, and to love, fear and obey God. From their love, the whole human race would spring and they in turn would continue

God's order: "Be fruitful and multiply."
Genesis 1:28

THE FALL OF MAN – GENESIS 3

The devil, Satan, in his desire for revenge on God, decided that the best way to hurt God was to hurt the beloved of His creation, Man and Woman.

He was successful, but only for a time. He beguiled them into disobeying God. They ate the one fruit in the garden that God had told them explicitly NOT to eat.

So God cast the man and his wife, Adam and Eve, out of the beautiful garden which He had created for them. Thereafter their work would be tiresome, laborious, and often unfulfilling.

God had given man a precious gift – free will. His desire was that they would love

Him of their own free will. He did not create robots; He created beings, like Himself.

God, by giving His creation love, has conferred His nature on us. The greatest human love becomes the love between man and wife. They have a child. The love for the child becomes as great as the love they have for each other. They have another child, and love the second as much as the first, and each other, and so on…

The child grows up and marries. The love he/she has for his parents is now also given to his mate, sometimes in even greater measure, and so on…

The Bible says that mankind became exceedingly wicked. Genesis 6:5

By now there were millions of people.

God destroyed the wicked in the Great Flood and started over, sparing only Noah and his family.

The Bible says "Noah was a just man, blameless in his generation." Genesis 6:9

So Noah and his family repopulated the earth. But, like before, mankind again left to their own devices, began going their own way, following their own desires, not God's.

The Bible mentions three basic sins of human nature: Pride, Lust and Greed. 1 John 2:16

Pride says, "I am Number One. My needs are most important."

Greed says, "Money will buy happiness."

Lust says, "Satisfy my physical desires."

These three have also been known as "money, sex and power"- or "gold, girls and glory."

GOD HAS A PLAN; GOD FINDS A MAN

Generations later, God found a man named Abraham, who was willing to follow God and obey His word. Because of his obedience, Abraham's descendants would be a people set apart for God's purpose: a nation who would obey Him, honor Him, follow Him and love Him - a nation who would demonstrate the kingdom of God on earth, a people God could bless and love.

Abraham so loved God and obeyed Him that he was called "God's friend." 2 Chronicles 20:7; Isaiah 41:8; James 2:23

Abraham's descendants would be a people set apart for God's purpose.

Most of the millions of people on earth by now (approximately 2,000 B.C.) did not love nor obey God. Most people want their own way and not be subject to rules.

Abraham was different. God saw his heart and knew Abraham would follow Him. God had a plan to give Abraham his own land, which happened to be the most beautiful place on earth.

Abraham's descendants were to dwell in that land.

He and his family, including his wife Sarah, left their homeland and followed God's leading. It was an arduous journey, but Abraham followed God obediently. .

God led them to the land of Canaan – the Bible calls it a "land of milk and honey."

In other words, a rich pastureland where there was plenty of room for their flocks and herds. Also there were many fruit trees, producing a wonderful place for bees to produce honey.

It was a land perfectly situated – wonderful climate, with the Mediterranean Sea on the west and the Jordan River on the east. It was ideal for commerce – for ships, caravans and by that time, established trade routes. It joined three continents.

By the way, California is at the same latitude as the land God gave Abraham. I think people in the United States would agree that California has the best climate in the nation.

Of course there were other peoples living in such a desirable land. Abraham was a peaceful man, and he and his family were allowed a place among the inhabitants.

One of his descendants was a great-grandson, Joseph. At that time Egypt was the dominant power in the world. Joseph became Pharaoh's second-in-command, and through his wisdom saved the rest of the world from famine.

Joseph's father Jacob and his eleven brothers, their wives, and their descendants all moved to Egypt in order to escape the ravages of the famine.

Four hundred years later, after Abraham's people had been sold into slavery, ruled by Egypt, God chose another man to lead them out of slavery and back into the land God gave to Abraham.

The man God chose for this enormous undertaking was Moses. Exodus 1:14

One of Joseph's brothers, Levi, had a great-grandson named Moses.

The Bible says that a king of Egypt arose who did not know Joseph and how he had saved Egypt. Generations passed. At that time Pharaoh felt threatened because of the multitudes of Israelites. So Pharaoh made slaves of them and placed them into harsh bondage. They served under cruel taskmasters.

They became cheap labor for Pharaoh, making bricks for the magnificent tombs he was building, in the shape of pyramids.

They were called Israelites, after the name of Abraham's grandson, Jacob, who was also called "Israel."

The Bible says that the people groaned under their burdens and cried out to God. Exodus 2:23

"So God heard their groaning, and God remembered His covenant with Abraham, with Isaac, and with Jacob." Exodus 2:24

This might raise a question in people's minds. Did God forget? Of course not. But when the Bible speaks of God remembering someone, it means He is about to act on their behalf.

"Then God remembered Noah…" Genesis 8:1

"God remembered Abraham" and rescued his nephew Lot from the destruction visited on Sodom and Gomorrah. Genesis 19:29

"Then God remembered Rachel, and God listened to her and opened her womb." Genesis 30:22

GOD IS ABOUT TO ACT!

GOD CHOOSES MOSES, WHO WILL BRING DELIVERANCE TO HIS PEOPLE.

Moses would lead them out of slavery and back to the land God gave to Abraham.

God sent Moses to Pharaoh, who with his brother Aaron, demanded he let His people go.

Through a series of miraculous plagues, Pharaoh finally yielded.

In Exodus 12 God gives specific instructions to Israel to save them from the plague that was to be visited upon Pharaoh and his citizens.

Exodus 12:2 – God declares that month to be the first month of the year for Israel. They would be starting a new calendar year. The first day of their year was in the Jewish month of Abib, roughly corresponding to our month of April. It was in the spring.

Every household was to select a young lamb, without blemish, on the 10th of Abib, to be an offering, and also a substitute, for the firstborn sons which the Lord was about to kill.

They would keep the lamb until the 14th, when it was to be slaughtered and eaten.

The days between Abib 10 and Abib 14 were for inspecting the lamb, to make sure it was perfect, without blemish.

On the 14th the lamb was to be killed. The blood was to be put on the sides and top of the doorframe of the house.

The lamb was to be roasted over a fire, and eaten with unleavened bread (bread made without yeast) and bitter herbs (possibly horseradish, celery and parsley).

All the Israelites were commanded to stay within the protection of their homes.

God would then kill every firstborn son of Egypt – as He warned Pharaoh He would do (Exodus 11:4-8).

Israel would then have to eat in haste, ready to move out quickly (Exodus 12:11).

God said, "On that same night I will pass through Egypt and strike down every firstborn of men and animals, and I will bring judgment on all the gods of Egypt. (Exodus 12:12.) The blood will be a sign on the houses where you are, and when I see the blood, I will PASS OVER you."

Moses and Aaron threatened the king that each firstborn son of every family in the land would die. When the king still refused, God carried out His threat.

Exodus 12:14 – God commands Israel to observe this day every year at this time.

THE FEASTS OF ISRAEL

God made a plan – a way for His people to remember His mercy, love and deliverance.

This is the story of the instigation of the seven feasts, or festivals of Israel.

Everyone loves feasts, or festivals…right?

Rabbi Samson Raphael Hirsch: "The catechism of the Jew consists of his calendar. This calendar, with its God-appointed times and memorials, is the one factor that has united the scattered nation. Wherever they are, faithful Jews the world over will pause in their routines to observe their holidays. The feasts reassure the Jew that there is a God in Israel who cares and watches over him and his people's destiny."

The feasts commemorated milestones in God's dealings with His people. They were designed to call to mind His faithfulness, power and goodness.

Beginning the festivals was the Sabbath. The Sabbath was not really included in the seven – but it needed a special place in the minds of the Israelites.

It is the fourth of the Ten Commandments found in Exodus 20:2-17.

The Sabbath is VERY important to God. Genesis 1 says that God created the world in six days and on the seventh He rested from all His work.

He insisted that His people rest on the Sabbath as well.

The penalty for not obeying God's command to rest was very severe.

The seven feasts of Israel are:

In the spring, which is also the time of the barley harvest:

Passover, Unleavened Bread, Sheaf of Firstfruits

In the summer, which is the time of the wheat harvest:

Pentecost – also called "The Feast of Weeks"

In the autumn, which is the time of the fruit harvest:

The Blowing of Trumpets, Day of Atonement, Feast of Tabernacles

Chapter One

THE PASSOVER

"When I see the blood, I will PASS OVER you." Exodus 12:13. In other words, God would spare His people from the plague - because of the blood on the door posts and the door frame of each house.

It could also mean that God would PASS OVER them like a giant eagle with the children safely under its wings. Psalm 91:1 says, "He who dwells in the secret place of the Most High shall abide under the shadow of the Almighty."

See also Psalm 17:8 "Hide me under the shadow of Your wings."

So the people of Israel were kept safe because God saw the blood on their doors, as the Egyptians suffered the death of each firstborn son.

God commanded Israel to celebrate the feast of Passover every year at this time, in the spring, to commemorate His great deliverance.

There was something very special in that first Passover meal. It nourished them so perfectly and completely that they ALL were perfectly healthy as they came out of Egypt! Elderly people must have been among them, as well as those who were sick, crippled and frail. Yet Psalm 105:37 says, "He also brought them out with silver and gold, and there was none feeble among them."

Israel kept the Passover, after the Passover in Egypt, in the second year after they had started their trek through the wilderness. Numbers 9:1-14. They didn't have to apply the blood on the doorposts of their houses anymore (that was to protect them while in Egypt). But they were to kill the ox or sheep or goat and to eat it as part of the ceremony, along with the bitter herbs. See God's instructions in Exodus 13.

Now - see how Jesus fulfilled the role as the Passover Lamb:

The Second Person of the Holy Trinity, the only Son of the Eternal Father, left the glories and bliss and happiness of heaven to step down to earth – to be imprisoned in time and space – placed as an embryo inside the womb of a young virgin girl – and to grow up as any other human being – all for the purpose of redeeming sinful people and bringing us back to our heavenly Father as His beloved children!!

What a wonder, what a privilege, what a blessing for all the sons and daughters of men!!

Just as the Passover lamb was to be set aside for four days, so Jesus was set aside four days (four thousand years). 2 Peter 3:8 says, "But, beloved, do not forget this one thing, that with the Lord one day is as a thousand years, and a thousand years as one day." See God's Plan of the Ages, Appendix 3.

On the day we call "Palm Sunday," Jesus rode into Jerusalem on a donkey. This fulfilled the Scripture in Zechariah 9:9. "Rejoice greatly, O daughter of Zion! Shout, O daughter of Jerusalem! Behold, your King is coming to you; He is just and having salvation, lowly and riding on a donkey, a colt, the foal of a donkey...He shall speak peace to the nations; His dominion shall be from sea to sea, and from the River to the ends of the earth."John 12:12

"The next day a great multitude...when they heard that Jesus was coming to Jerusalem, took branches of palm trees and went out to meet Him, and cried out:

> "Hosanna! Blessed is He who comes in the name of the Lord! The King of Israel!"

They also shouted the verse from Zechariah: "Fear not, daughter of Zion; behold your King is coming, sitting on a donkey's colt." John 12:15

Jesus then celebrated the Passover meal with His disciples. John 13:2-5. "And supper being ended… (He) rose from supper and laid aside His garments, took a towel and girded Himself. After that He poured water into a basin and began to wash His disciples' feet and to wipe them with the towel with which He was girded."

Jesus was teaching them a lesson about serving one another. He wanted to make them understand that the important thing was not what others could do for them, but what we can do for others. And so it is for all of His disciples throughout the world and throughout the ages. Life is not just about us.

I remember the old Sunday school acronym: JOY – first Jesus, then Others, then You. If we can keep this proper order in our lives, it results in JOY!

John 12:32: (Jesus said) "And I, if I be lifted up from the earth (on a cross), will draw all peoples to Myself." This He said, signifying by what death He would die.

> In John 1:29, we read how Jesus appeared as the Lamb of God, the only begotten Son of Father God.

John the Baptist saw Jesus headed his way and called out to all those around, "Behold the Lamb of God, who takes away the sin of the world!"

Just as the first Passover lamb, in Moses time, had to be inspected for four days to make sure it was without blemish, note:

Jesus was examined four days to see if He was fit:

1. By the Herodians, Matthew 22:16
2. By the Sadducees, Matthew 22:23
3. By the Pharisees, Matthew 22:34

4. By the High Priest, then before the Roman governor, Pontius Pilate, John 18:28.

The final pronouncement – made by the highest authority in the land, Pontius Pilate, was:

"I FIND NO FAULT IN HIM AT ALL!" John 18:38; 19:4, 6.

Yes, Jesus perfectly fulfills our substitute as the Passover Lamb of God! No blemish at all!

So Jesus, my Lord and Savior, was totally fit to be slaughtered and to die the most horrible and painful death imaginable…all for the sake of us sinful human beings… and only because of HIS precious blood… all who consider that blood precious…all who acknowledge that we are totally unfit and unworthy of such amazing grace, can claim our inheritance as a child of God.

And that is what Passover is all about.

Because the Lamb of God is our substitute to protect us all from the plague and pain of eternal death, ALL WHO WILL ACCEPT HIM AS THEIR SUBSTITUTE can look forward to eternity in heaven.

Blissful eternal life!!

Chapter Two

SACRIFICES AND OFFERINGS

Leviticus 1-9

From earliest history people have been inclined to sacrifice. Cain and Abel, the first sons born to Adam and Eve, offered their sacrifices to God. Genesis 4:1-4.

In practically every culture, to sacrifice seems as natural to people as to pray. It indicates a felt need of dependence on God.

1. They were expressions of thanksgiving and reverence.

2. People indicated a felt need of propitiation (atonement) and substitution for sin.
3. People wanted to secure God's favor and blessing.

God intended to address those needs.

THE FIVE SACRIFICES

As part of every festival God commanded certain sacrifices. There were five, and each had a specific purpose.

THE BURNT OFFERING. Leviticus 1

It was an expression of thanksgiving and dedication.

> The offerer was to bring an offering from either the herd (bull or ox), or from the flock (sheep or goat). It had to be male, and without spot or blemish. If they could not afford one of the first two, they were permitted

to bring a turtle dove or young pigeon. That was what Mary and Joseph brought when Jesus was dedicated. Luke 2:24.

It represented complete dedication of one's life to the Lord. See Romans 12:1.

As part of the offering, wine was to be poured out. Wine represented joy. It also represented the blood of Christ.

THE MEAL OFFERING. Leviticus 2

It was offered for the purpose of giving back to God a portion of the earthly blessings bestowed on them.

It was to be baked of fine flour and salt. It must have no leaven or honey.

The meal offering was always accompanied by a drink offering of wine.

THE PEACE OFFERING. Leviticus 3

A. It was a thank offering – a recognition of unmerited and/or unexpected blessings. Leviticus 7:12-15.

B. It could be a votive offering, for the purpose of paying a vow. Leviticus 7:16.

C. A freewill offering – an expression of love for God. Leviticus 22:18-25.

No defects were accepted!

The purpose was to celebrate the fellowship and peace already made with God.

Ephesians 2:14 says Christ is our peace!

THE SIN OFFERING. Leviticus 4, 5

A. It was for when a person, a ruler, or the High Priest sinned unintentionally.

B. Or, if the whole congregation sinned unintentionally. An example is the case of Achan, in Joshua 7.

It was to be offered when the sinner became aware of the sin. Leviticus 4:14; 4:23; 4:28.

Leviticus 5 gives more instances of unintentional sins.

If a person sinned intentionally, or presumptuously, see

Numbers 15:30-36.

THE TRESPASS/GUILT OFFERING.
Leviticus 6:1-7

This was when an individual committed an offense against another member of the congregation. For example: Losing something that was entrusted to them for safekeeping. Leviticus 6:1-7

There was always restitution to be made to the offended party.

Chapter Three

THE FEAST OF UNLEAVENED BREAD, Leviticus 23:6

Part of the Passover – but important enough to be listed separately, was Unleavened Bread.

It began on the 15th day of the month of Abib and lasted seven days. They were to eat only bread made without leaven, or yeast. In fact, no leaven was to be found anywhere in their house. They would use lamps and search diligently in every nook and cranny to make sure there was no trace of leaven.

Why? Think what leaven, or yeast, does. It makes bread rise. It puffs up! See 1 Corinthians 5:2. Also see 1 Corinthians 13:4.

There is no place for pride or self-promotion in the life of the believer.

Just as the Passover prefigures a person's conversion to Christ, so Unleavened Bread prefigures their sanctification – in other words, their life of holiness lived for Christ.

When a believer undergoes water baptism they declare themselves to be entering a life dedicated to Christ.

Each household was to search diligently throughout their house to make sure there was not even a crumb of leavened bread around.

This is a picture of sanctification, or holiness. 1 Corinthians 5:7 says, "Purge out the old leaven, that you may be a new lump (of dough)."

This symbolizes the believer's new life and new start. It has long been associated with the believer's water baptism. Colossians 2:12 "Buried with Him in baptism…" Also see 1 Corinthians 10:1,2

To Israel it meant the actual passing through the Red Sea, which forever separated them from their enemies, the Egyptians.

In a Christian's water baptism, he/she is to be forever separated from their enemies, the things of the world which pull on one. The sins of the flesh are strong, but water baptism will enable the believer to leave them behind forever.

As Israel's first Passover taught them the necessity of a lamb's blood, shed to deliver them from their bondage to slavery – so the festival of Unleavened Bread taught them they were to live a life of holiness to God.

They were fully delivered from Egypt's bondage when they went through the Red Sea – and rose from the sea with their enemies dead and powerless behind them. Exodus 14:15-31. See also 1 Corinthians 10:1-3

After John the Baptist identified Jesus as the true Lamb of God, he then baptized Him. Jesus went on to live a life of true holiness before His Father.

As He lay in the tomb for three days and nights, there was no leaven in Him. There was never anything in Him that puffs up. Even though He is the God eternal, He laid it all aside to be our substitute.

Chapter Four

THE SHEAF OF FIRSTFRUITS

Leviticus 23:9-14

And the Lord spoke to Moses, saying, "Speak to the children of Israel, and say to them: 'When you come into the land which I give to you, and reap its harvest, then you shall bring a sheaf of the firstfruits of your harvest to the priest. He shall wave the sheaf before the Lord, to be accepted on your behalf; on the day after the Sabbath the priest shall wave it."

God goes on to say that they must offer the sheaf to the Lord before they themselves eat the grain/bread.

It was in the book of Joshua 5:10-12 where we read that Israel first celebrated Passover, Unleavened Bread and the Sheaf of Firstfruits, having finally arrived in the Promised Land.

God wanted to teach His people GRATITUDE.

Gratitude is one of the most important traits a person can have. How many of you have been severely hurt and disappointed by someone's ingratitude? I know I have.

In order to show their gratitude to God, He commanded them to first offer a sheaf of the first produce of their crops to Him.

This festival is alluded to in Matthew 27 at the moment of Christ's death…"the bodies of many holy people who had died were raised to life." Matthew 27:52-53. In 1 Corinthians 15:20-23, Christ is called the "Firstfruits of those who slept"…in other words, the righteous ones who had died – but when Christ rose they rose with Him.

"But now Christ is risen from the dead, and has become the firstfruits of those who have fallen asleep. For since by man came death, by Man also came the resurrection of the dead. For as in Adam all die, even so in Christ all shall be made alive. But each one in their own order: Christ the firstfruits, afterward those who are Christ's at His coming."

Many people believe that believers have always gone directly into the presence of God in heaven when they die, even in the Old Testament. Jesus told a story which seems to say otherwise. In Luke 16:19 Jesus tells about a very rich man, and a very poor beggar named Lazarus. Lazarus was so poor he wanted to eat only of the crumbs of bread that fell from the rich man's table. But the rich man was selfish and didn't care anything about the poor.

Later the poor man died and was carried by angels into Abraham's bosom. Later the rich man died and was in torment in Hades. Luke 16:19-23.

The remarkable thing is that the rich man could see Lazarus in a pleasant place while he himself was in agony. There was a great gulf between them so that neither could get to the other.

This suggests sort of a "holding place" before the Cross, or before Jesus actually died and rose. When Jesus rose from the grave and ascended into heaven, He brought the righteous dead with Him.

That is why Jesus is called "Firstfruits" in 1 Corinthians 15:23, followed by all the righteous dead who lived before His resurrection.

From that moment on, all believers in Jesus Christ have risen to heaven to be with Him forever.

Chapter Five

PENTECOST – also called THE FEAST OF WEEKS

MT. SINAI
BEWARE!!

Leviticus 23:15-22

Specifically Israel celebrated the giving of the Law by God, on the top of Mt. Sinai – fifty days (or seven weeks) after they came out of Egypt.

Israel took great pride in having God's law—they even prided themselves on being the only nation to have it. Psalm 147:19, 20; Romans 9:4.

Fifty days after Passover, when Israel was finally released from her bondage to Egypt, God called to Moses from the top of Mount Sinai, then spoke to all Israel. He had already saved them from bondage by the blood of the lamb, but before He would allow them to enter the land He had promised them, He gave them instructions on how to live. Exodus 19:4-6.

And the Lord said to Moses "Thus you shall say to the house of Jacob and tell the children of Israel: You have seen what I did to the Egyptians, and how I bore you on eagles' wings and brought you to Myself. Now therefore, if you will indeed obey My voice and keep My covenant, then you shall be a special treasure to Me above all people, for all the earth is mine. And you shall be to Me a kingdom of priests and a holy nation."

Exodus 19:16: Then it came to pass on the third day, in the morning, that there were thunderings and lightnings, and a thick cloud on the mountain; and the sound of the trumpet was very loud, so that all the people who were in the camp trembled. And Moses brought the people out of the camp to meet with God, and they stood at the foot of the mountain. Now Mount Sinai was completely in smoke, because the Lord descended upon it in fire. Its smoke ascended like the smoke of a furnace, and the whole mountain quaked greatly. And when the blast of the trumpet sounded long and became louder and louder, Moses spoke, and God answered him by voice. Then the Lord came down upon Mount Sinai, on the top of the mountain. And the Lord called Moses to the top of the mountain, and Moses went up.

A very fearsome event for Israel!

So terrifying was it to Israel that they begged Moses to listen to God instead of them hearing Him themselves.

God gave them the Ten Commandments and the rest of His laws, which would teach them how to live in His ways and principles. These laws would set them apart and make them different from all the other nations of the world. All of these laws are set forth in Exodus, Leviticus Numbers and Deuteronomy. Deuteronomy means "The second giving of the law."

The Law was Israel's pride and joy, considered their most treasured heritage.

Before we can enter all that God has for us, we must learn to live the way He wants us to. In Ezekiel 36:26, the Father promised to place His Spirit within His people, causing them to walk according to His statutes (laws). When they learned to walk in obedience, THEN He said His people would live under His blessing. This was the purpose at Sinai, but this was also the purpose in Acts 2. The Holy Spirit dwells with us to teach us of God's ways and to help us with our weaknesses, so that we might be prepared to enter into all the blessings He has for us. Romans 8:26 says, "Likewise the Spirit also helps in our weaknesses. For we do not know what we should pray for as we ought, but the Spirit Himself makes intercession for us…"

Fifty days after Jesus was crucified on the festival of Passover and subsequently rose from the dead and ascended into heaven, as His disciples watched – came the Jewish Festival of Pentecost.

Jews from all over the known world had assembled in Jerusalem to celebrate Pentecost.

On that day the events in Acts 2 took place:

The disciples were assembled together, praying, as Jesus had commanded (Luke 24:49).

Jews who were living in other countries besides Israel, and who spoke the languages of the countries where they lived – were amazed when the disciples came pouring out of the place where they were, proclaiming the wonderful works of God in all the different languages of those attending the festival! Acts 2:1-14

From this beginning, the Church began to grow. This is all set forth in the book of Acts.

Here we see the first four Festivals of Israel – with their corresponding fulfillment in the life of Jesus Christ:

Passover in the Spring:

The lamb was slain so Israel could be released from Egyptian bondage.

Jesus was slain as the Lamb of God (John 1:29) so people everywhere can be released from bondage to sin and the devil.

Fifty days later, Pentecost in the summer – came the giving of God's Law to His people to teach them how they should live.

Fifty days later, after Jesus was crucified, risen and ascended into heaven, the Holy Spirit gave the law of Christ to His church, to empower them to live according to His will, and to do His works.

So began the dispensation of the Church Age....

Chapter Six

THE CHURCH AGE – A BRIEF OVERVIEW

Rome ruled the world and forbade serving another king besides Caesar. The emperor Nero Caesar was responsible for the martyrdom of Paul and possibly Peter.

The Roman general Titus destroyed Jerusalem in 70 A.D.

The church grew rapidly for 300 years as it was being persecuted.

In 326 A.D. the Roman emperor Constantine became a Christian.

Persecution of Christians ceased.

The church became governed by appointees of Rome. They were called "popes," and were given great authority in the church.

1. The Baptism in the Holy Spirit was no longer sought as empowerment for ministry.
2. Water Baptism was administered by sprinkling not immersion.
3. People no longer relied on the blood sacrifice of Jesus Christ for their salvation. Instead they believed salvation was attained by observing man-made laws:
   a. Reciting prayers, with beads.
   b. Paying fees (called "indulgences") to church leaders.
   c. Mary began to be elevated even higher than Jesus, as the focus of worship.

This continued for centuries, up to the time of Martin Luther in the 1500's. Luther was a pious, God-seeking monk, who knew there had to be something more in his Christian experience.

As he prayed and sought God, he read a verse in the Bible: "The just shall live by faith." Romans 1:17; Habakkuk 2:4.

This revelation set Luther free from his self-imposed struggle to please God.

He must let them know!

Luther posted his "95 Theses," as they have become known, on the door of the church - and was persecuted. But a light now shone in the darkness.

God was going to bring the light of truth back to His people!

People cannot be saved by what <u>they</u> do, but by what Christ has already done – bought our salvation through the shedding of His own precious blood.

In the 18th century John Wesley, a dedicated minister of the Baptist fellowship, realized true water baptism was administered by submersion, as practiced in the early church.

Wesley also was grieved by the lack of holy living among Christians.

Followers of Luther did not like this teaching, so they persecuted Wesley's followers, just as followers of the Popes persecuted Lutherans.

In 1906, God was ready to restore the truth of the Baptism in the Holy Spirit, along with the speaking in other languages.

All these revivals were sparked by believers who kept on wanting more of what the early church had. They wanted passion, eagerness, and the excitement of doing the work of Christ.

In 1906 came what is known as the "Azusa Street Revival." (See "God, Gold and Glory," pages 99-127, by Henry Falany).

A group of young ladies were meeting regularly for prayer. A preacher known as "Daddy" Seymour was directed by God to go to the place where the girls were meeting. They rented a barn in Los Angeles, and began to have regular services. It wasn't long before they got the attention of many others – those who were tired of dead church life – and wanted the enthusiasm of the early church.

Revival took place in a big way! People were filled with the Holy Spirit – speaking in other tongues and seeing miracles and great healings take place. More than once the Fire Department came because they saw "flames coming from the roof"! It was the fire of the Holy Spirit! Witnesses said they saw flames coming down from heaven to meet those coming from the building!

Astonishing miracles took place in those meetings. Pastor Falany tells the story of a one-armed man whose missing arm grew out before the eyes of the hundreds of those watching! There were other such miracles of body parts growing back as people watched. Many who were in wheel chairs got out of their chairs and walked. Broken bones snapped into place! I urge you to read Pastor Falany's account for yourself. So amazing!

So the truth of the Baptism with the Holy Spirit came back into the church! A new day had dawned! It rapidly spread throughout the whole world – people came to Azusa Street and then went back to their own churches to tell of the wonders.

Another event took place in 1906, the San Francisco earthquake. Buildings were destroyed and lives were lost. There was widespread fear. God uses times like these to get people's attention!

As before, the followers of John Wesley did not like this new move of God in the church. So they argued against it then, persecuting those who spoke in other tongues, and still do.

I can personally say that my own life was changed forever when I encountered this for myself.

Following the pattern which has been going on for centuries – four festivals of the Lord being fulfilled and enacted by the Church of Jesus Christ – should we expect the other three feasts to be fulfilled also?

Yes! The purpose of this book is to set forth that which many believers are about to see fulfilled in our day...

Chapter Seven

THE FEAST OF THE BLOWING OF TRUMPETS

Leviticus 23:23; Numbers 10:10. See also Psalm 81:3.

The Jews call this feast "Rosh Hashanah." It is the Jewish New Year. "Rosh" means "head." So it can be translated as "Head of the Year."

Some believe God created the world on this day.

Some say that Abraham offered up his son Isaac as a sacrifice to God on this day. Genesis 22:1-19.

Trumpets were to be blown all day long. This suggests that it was a noisy feast! Does God like noise? Apparently He does!

Or does He prefer that people sit quietly in their church pews, without enthusiasm? I don't think so.

In times of revival there have always been great praise and worship; it is a natural response to God's presence in our midst. But at this particular revival it was all about praise and worship!

Note Ezekiel 37:7: There was a noise – a rattling sound, as the dead and dried up bones came together!

Could this be referring to the Church of Jesus Christ? What do you think? Or, how about Israel – back in her land but in unbelief?

In 1948, two great events took place. One is widely known throughout the world:

1. Israel became a sovereign nation for the first time since they were dispersed after their temple was destroyed in 70 A.D.
2. The second event – not that widely known – was a revival in the church that took place in Canada.

    A group of ministers met there for the purpose of seeking God – what His will was for them as leaders in their churches. There was a consensus among them – something they felt God was speaking to them about – that a great new move of God was on the horizon.

They agreed about several things God was saying to them:

a. Praise and worship were to be intensified. One of the foremost pastors who had gathered there received new insight into Psalm 22:3 – "God inhabits the praises of His people." In other words, not only is God pleased when we praise Him, but He Himself comes to dwell with us! We can sense His palpable presence – both when a group praises Him, as well as when any of us individually praises Him!

I can verify myself that this has been my experience again and again! Talk about a high! No high on intoxicating drinks can begin to approach the high you get when the Holy Spirit moves through you!

The people who met in Canada agreed that the Pentecostal movement of 1906 had grown cold and that the Church had lost its fervency. In particular, there were a group of Bible college students who were longing for a fresh move of the Holy Spirit. Ministers from all over Canada and the United States heard about what was going on and went to see for themselves. Pastor Reg Layzell of Glad Tidings Temple in Vancouver, B.C. was one of the leaders at the gathering. He spent three months in intense prayer. Then in order to spread the message he sponsored annual summer camp meetings at Crescent Beach, B. C.

Our former pastors, Ernest and Joy Gentile, were among those who attended. They were just 20 years old and already pastoring a church in Spokane, Washington.

To quote Pastor Gentile, "We were not disappointed, just overwhelmed. The people gathered at the altars for an hour before the regular service started. The prayer was fervent, anointed and totally impressive to us. The worship services were thunderous with praise for sometimes more than an hour...the people employed psalmic worship in a natural, free-flowing style. With upraised hands they praised the Lord audibly. Gifts of the Spirit functioned. (See 1 Corinthians 12)."

In times of revival there have always been great praise and worship. It is a natural response to God's presence in our midst. But at the revival of 1948 it was all about praise and worship!

They called themselves "Latter Rain" because of references in Hosea 6:4; Joel 2:23; and Zechariah 10:1. When Israel was obedient the Lord sent rain on the land. But in times of rebellion rain was withheld. Since Israel was mostly an agricultural nation, they depended on the seasonal rains – called "The former rain and the latter rain." The former rain fell at the beginning of the year and the latter rain fell at the end. Especially the latter rain was desired to bring in the climax of the harvest season.

Just as each revival was disdained and rejected by the one just preceding it, so the Latter Rain revival was rejected by the Pentecostals. I had a friend in our church in San Jose (a "latter rain" church) who told me her Pentecostal mother warned her to "stay away from Latter Rain." "Latter rain" was used as a term of disdain by the ones who did not want to move on with God. I am so glad our Pastor Gentile's mindset was to embrace all that God has for us! Hebrews 4:1 warns us about stopping short and failing to enter into the rest He wants us to enjoy.

Another verse was spotlighted during this time of seeking God in Canada: 1Timothy 4:14 – "Neglect not the not the gift that is in you, that was given you by prophecy by the laying on of hands by the presbytery." The presbytery were the leaders, or elders, of the local churches. These gifts are for the purpose of bringing clarity to each believer of how we fit into the body of Christ. Gifts were also imparted at the time of the laying on of hands. These gifts and ministries are found in Romans 12 as well as 1 Corinthians 12.

See Hebrews 6:1-2. These two verses lay out great Christian truths, which all but disappeared during the Dark Ages.

Salvation by faith restored during time of Martin Luther.

Doctrine of baptisms:

Water baptism and sanctification –
John Wesley

Baptism with the Holy Spirit in 1906

Laying on of hands,

Resurrection of the dead.

Eternal judgment.

Chapter Eight

THE TIMES OF THE GENTILES

Throughout the centuries, God has used Israel's festivals to show us what He is doing – in the Church, in Israel, and the rest of the world.

Toward the end they have gotten closer together. Have you noticed?

To illustrate, Pentecost and Trumpets were both fulfilled in the previous century.

The next major festival will be the Day of Atonement (Yom Kippur). Many Christians believe that will be the day Christ returns to take His people to heaven to be with Him. 1 Thessalonians 4:15-18.

There is another sign of Christ's return, when His disciples were asking Him about it.

There is an astounding prophecy in Luke 21:24. Jesus is foretelling both the destruction of the beautiful and magnificent temple in Jerusalem – and His return to earth.

"For there will be great distress in the land, and wrath upon this people." Luke 21:23.

Luke 21:24: "And they will fall by the edge of the sword, and be led away captive into all nations, and JERUSALEM WILL BE TRAMPLED BY GENTILES UNTIL THE TIMES OF THE GENTILES ARE FULFILLED."

This raises two questions:

1. What did Jesus mean when He referred to "the times of the Gentiles"?

2. Is Jerusalem still being trampled by the Gentiles?

The "times of the Gentiles" refers to the time when God turned His attention away from Israel to the rest of the world – non-Jews, called "Gentiles."

We see that situation throughout Church history, as the Church of Jesus Christ became God's focus. Although at first the church consisted mostly of Jews, it grew mightily throughout the Church Age. Even at the time of the Apostle Paul, not long after Jesus had returned to heaven, there were many non-Jews, or Gentiles, in the church.

The Apostle Paul confirmed this when he said that God would send him to the Gentiles to preach the good news of Jesus. Acts 22:21. This enraged the Jews who were listening to him.

Has Jerusalem been trampled by the Gentiles since Jesus uttered this prophecy?

When Israel was serving God and being obedient to His will, God kept their enemies at bay. But whenever they were disobedient to His will God allowed their enemies access to them. He warned them of this again and again. See Deuteronomy 28 where God outlines blessings for obedience and severe and dreadful punishments for disobedience.

We see this throughout the period when judges governed Israel, then during the period of the kings. There were godly kings, of whom David was paramount, and wicked kings.

The last king to reign in Jerusalem was Zedekiah in 586 B.C.

In 586 B.C. Jerusalem fell to King Nebuchadnezzar of Babylon. Most of the people had died during the siege, or killed after Babylonian forces broke through the walls – a sad time indeed for Israel – but God had warned them through their prophets again and again of what would happen if they continued their disobedience.

So the city was trampled and laid waste until the time of the great reformer, Nehemiah, who led a group of volunteers to restore the city's walls.

The city was rebuilt, but without the grandeur of the past.

For a while, God favored Israel with peace during the times of Esther, Ezra and Nehemiah. That was a time of revival when Israel obeyed God. It was during the reigns of Xerxes and Artaxerxes. Israel was no longer a sovereign nation, but was subject to Gentile rulers.

Different countries with different kings pummeled the city – Babylon, Persia, Greece, Syria, Egypt, Rome…. (you can read about this period in the book of Daniel).

Jesus was born during the reign of Augustus Caesar.

He died during the reign of Tiberius Caesar.

During the Church Age – AD 70 up to the present era, the city has been subjected to Gentile cruelty: Roman emperors, Mohammed followers, Turks, Spain, Egypt, Palestine…

Chapter Nine

JERUSALEM

Let us pause to consider what has often been called "The City of David."

David was known as "a man after God's own heart." God Himself gave him that name – 1 Samuel 13:14. That was because David had many of the qualities that God Himself has – kindness, justice, mercy, a sense of righteousness. David also was a worshiper of God, he was also very courageous and brave. He put others' interests ahead of his own (2 Samuel 15:19. Of course many people know about his lapse into sin when he allowed temptation to overtake him. David did a terrible thing – but the lesson is that God will have mercy on us if we truly repent and turn back to Him. God will have mercy, but the effects of our sin remain. See 2 Samuel 12:7-23; Psalm 51.

King David and his forces captured the city of Jerusalem in approximately 1,000 BC. There were still strongholds of Canaanite people in the land of Israel, and the Jebusites held the city of Jerusalem. It was called "Jebus." It was only twelve acres in length, but could well defend itself against attack because of its situation. It had walls atop steep canyons and shafts reaching underground water sources. It was ideal as a fortress when David and his army captured it. 2 Samuel 5:7-8. "Then David dwelt in the stronghold and called it "'The City of David.' "

In 1 Chronicles 21 God directed David to build Him an altar on this site.

Psalm 132:13-14 – "For the Lord has chosen Zion; He has desired it for His dwelling place."

"This is My resting place forever; here I will dwell, for I have desired it."

Later, after Israel became divided, Jerusalem remained the capital of the southern kingdom of Judah.

Chapter Ten

THE DIVIDED KINGDOM

God told David in 2 Samuel 7:16 that his throne would be established forever.

God was pleased that David desired to build Him a temple. He told David that he would not build it, but his son Solomon would.

SOLOMON'S REIGN

Solomon did indeed build the magnificent temple, and for a while obeyed God. But a time came when he was old, and had many wives, and his wives persuaded him to worship their idols. Solomon gave in and thus began his downfall. 1 Kings 11:11. Also see Deuteronomy 17:17 where God warns Israel that their king "must not multiply wives for himself, lest his heart turn away…"

God further told Solomon that he would tear the kingdom away from him, not in his reign, but during the reign of his son. He said it was for the sake of David his father that He would show this kindness to David's son. 1 Kings 11:12.

This happened after Solomon died, and his son Rehoboam reigned. All the tribes of Israel except Judah and Benjamin revolted. A former servant named Jeroboam was appointed by a prophet of the Lord to be king of the ten other tribes. 1 Kings 11:29-43.

Thus, the kingdom became divided in two: the kingdom of Israel to the north, and the kingdom of Judah to the south.

The king of the northern kingdom, Jeroboam, decided it would be too much trouble for his people to go to the temple in Jerusalem to worship, as they were supposed to do. He was especially concerned that his people would desert him and go back to King Rehoboam of Judah. So he had two calf idols made of gold, and set them up as objects of worship. They were in two different places in Israel – one in Bethel and the other in Dan. The Bible says that "this became a sin…" Jeroboam did other things his own way and not God's, setting himself up for failure and judgment. This is in 1 Kings 12:28-33.

The kingdom of Israel and the kingdom of Judah fought often fought with each other. 2 Chronicles 13:2. 1 Chronicles 13:18 says, "The children of Judah prevailed because they relied on the Lord God of their fathers."

The kings of the northern kingdom included Ahab and Jezebel, whom many are familiar with. The great prophets Elijah and Elisha prophesied to the northern kingdom, warning them again and again to obey God. But none of the northern kings heeded them. In 2 Kings 17, we read that the king of Assyria besieged Samaria (the capital of the northern kingdom) for three years. "In the ninth year of Hoshea, the king of Assyria took Samaria and carried Israel away to Assyria. "Therefore the Lord was very angry with Israel and removed them from His sight; there was none left but the tribe of Judah alone." 2 Kings 17:18.

It was in 721 BC that the northern kingdom of Israel fell.

The southern kingdom of Judah had some godly kings – such as Uzziah, Jehoshaphat, Hezekiah, Josiah… There were times of revival under such kings.

The major prophets Isaiah, Jeremiah, Ezekiel, and Daniel prophesied in a chronological order in relationship to when Jerusalem fell: Isaiah, before the fall; Jeremiah during the fall; Ezekiel, after the fall and while in Babylon; Daniel, after the fall and while serving first King Nebuchadnezzar and then King Darius.

The last king of Judah was Zedekiah, who came to such a sad end. 2 Kings 25:4-7. Nebuchadnezzar of Babylon besieged the city for three years until they broke through the walls and carried the people away to Babylon.

Not only did they carry the people of Judah away to Babylon, they also burned and destroyed the magnificent temple that King Solomon had built. They took articles and furnishings of gold, silver and bronze as plunder.

"Thus Judah was carried away captive from its own land." 2 Kings 25:21

The southern kingdom of Judah was not known as "Israel" anymore – that was the name of the northern kingdom. The people of Judah were then called "Jews" – short for Judah. In the restoration books of Ezra, Nehemiah and Esther, they were called "Jews" almost exclusively.

In Jesus' encounter with the Samaritan woman, the woman wonders that Jesus would even talk to a Samaritan, since they had been at enmity all these years. See John 4. The Samaritans were called by the name of their capital city, Samaria. The woman called Jesus a "Jew," which of course He was, being descended from the southern kingdom.

Chapter Eleven

THE SIX-DAY WAR

As has been already noted, the "Times of the Gentiles" began when God turned His attention away from Israel to the rest of the world.

Now, the prophecy by Jesus in Luke 21:24 has been brought to the forefront.

In 1967, Israel made a bold move and invaded Egypt in what has been called "The Six-Day War." In that war Israel took back lands which were still being "trampled by Gentiles":

It began on June 5, 1967 and ended on June 10, 1967 – war with the Arab states of Egypt, Jordan and Syria.

Egyptian president Gamal Nasser ordered Egyptian forces to advance onto the Sinai Peninsula, where they expelled a U.N. peacekeeping force that had been guarding the border of Israel for over a decade.

Nasser continued to rattle the saber. On May 22, 1967, he banned shipping from the Straits of Tiran, the sea passage connecting the Red Sea and the Gulf of Aqaba.

By the end of the day, however, on June 5, 1967, Israeli pilots had won full control of the skies over the Middle East. In less than a week, Israel had captured the Sinai Peninsula and the Gaza Strip from Egypt, the West Bank and East Jerusalem from Jordan, and the Golan Heights from Syria.

(Sources: Wikipedia, The History Channel)

So the question is....did this war fulfill Jesus' prophecy in Luke 21:24? There are many, including the author, who think it did.

I had a mentor, who was also a very learned and astute Bible teacher, named Anna. She and I were discussing that prophecy in Luke. She told me at the time just after that war that she read the prophecy, and before her eyes the verse in the Bible became **bolded**. It was as if the Lord was affirming her!

If it did indeed fulfill Jesus' prophecy, then we are definitely nearing the time of His return.

While there are still battles between Israel and her enemies, it seems as if Jerusalem is no longer being trampled.

I have friends who have lived in Jerusalem for many years. I called my friend recently to ask her about this. She answered my question about Jerusalem being trampled at the present time. She said emphatically "No!"

So...the times of the Gentiles are over!

The fact that five of the seven feasts have been fulfilled, with Number 4 and Number 5 being fulfilled in our time, is another remarkable indication that we are nearing that momentous day!

Chapter Twelve

THE DAY OF ATONEMENT

The sixth feast is "The Day of Atonement" –
also called by the Jews "Yom Kippur."

It was the day in Israel's history when once a year, in the autumn, they would fast and pray and beseech God to forgive their sins. It was held ten days after Trumpets. Those days between Rosh Hashanah and Yom Kippur were known as "Ten Days of Awe."

Leviticus 23:26:-32: "And the Lord spoke to Moses, saying: "Also the tenth day of this seventh month shall be the Day of Atonement. It shall be a holy convocation for you; you shall afflict your souls (fast), and offer an offering made by fire to the Lord. And you shall do no work on that same day, for it is the Day of Atonement, to make atonement for you before the Lord your God. For any person who is not afflicted in soul on that same day shall be cut off from his people. And any person who does any work on that same day, that person I will destroy from among his people..."

Leviticus 16:2: And the Lord said to Moses: "Tell Aaron your brother not to come at just any time into the Holy Place inside the veil, before the mercy seat which is on the ark, lest he die; for I will appear in the cloud above the mercy seat."

First the High Priest was commanded to offer a sacrifice for himself. Leviticus 16:3

Then he was to take two goats. He was to cast lots for the goats. One goat was chosen to be slain as an offering for the sins of the people. The other goat was to be the scapegoat and was to be driven into the wilderness and released.

Aaron was to take a censor of burning coals from the altar before the Lord, and in his hands sweet incense, and bring it behind the veil where the mercy seat rested upon the Ark of the Covenant.

Then he was to kill the goat which was for the people and also bring its blood inside the veil and sprinkle it before the mercy seat and on the mercy seat.

The High Priest was to go alone into the tent of meeting. There was to be no other person in there with him. All the hope of the entire nation was pinned onto that one man. If he failed anywhere along the way in carrying out his obligations there could be no atonement made for his people.

Consider Jesus during His arrest and crucifixion – alone, forsaken by His friends and at last, even by His Father Himself. On Him alone depended the fate of the entire world – every obligation of the Law He had to fulfill perfectly.

Jesus became the goat of the sin offering when He took upon Himself the sins of all the world (2 Corinthians 5:21; Isaiah 53:6;

1 Peter 2:24; Hebrews 9:26,28). His blood made complete atonement with God for humankind. See also Hebrews 9.

Definition of "scapegoat": One who is blamed for the wrongdoing, mistakes, or faults of others…"

This is what Jesus was, as He took upon Himself the wrongdoing, mistakes, and faults of everyone who had ever lived and who will ever live.

The fact the scapegoat was released into the wilderness tells us that we are free because of Jesus. People are set free because of what Jesus did – but they also need someone to guide them out of the wilderness. This is where the Church comes in.

When Jesus took His last breath, hanging on the cross, some remarkable events took place. According to Matthew 27:51-53:

1. The heavy curtain in the temple in Jerusalem ripped in two from top to bottom.

   This was the curtain that was in front of the "Most Holy Place" – which could only be entered once a year on this day, Yom Kippur, and that only by the High Priest.

2. There was a great earthquake,
3. And the rocks were split,
4. And the graves were opened,
5. And many bodies of the saints who had fallen asleep were raised;
6. And coming out of the graves after His resurrection, they went into the holy city and appeared to many.

Matthew 27:54 – So when the centurion and those who were with him, who were guarding Jesus, saw the earthquake and the things that had happened, they feared greatly, saying: "TRULY, THIS WAS THE SON OF GOD!"

When the heavy veil in the temple was torn in two, it signified that now, upon Christ's death, *the way is open for all to come into the holy presence of God.* God the Father invites all who accept the blood of

Jesus Christ as our atonement for sin to come to Him.

Chapter Thirteen

THE FEAST OF TABERNACLES

ALSO CALLED THE FEAST OF BOOTHS, HARVEST, INGATHERING

This was the last of the Festivals of the Lord – the seventh feast in the seventh month, lasting seven days.

Leviticus 23:33-34; Numbers 29:12-39; Deuteronomy 16:13-15

It was called the Feast of Tabernacles, or Booths, because the Israelites were commanded to live in booths (shelters made of leafy boughs of trees) during it. It was to remind them of the forty long years in the wilderness, when God dwelt with them with a glory that was visible —a pillar of cloud by day and a pillar of fire by night. The leafy booths were to remind them of God's protection and provision during that time. He sheltered them from the heat by the pillar of cloud by day, and from the cold by a pillar of fire by night.

It was called the Feast of Harvest, or Ingathering, because Israel celebrated the ingathering of fruit (figs, olives, grapes) then, in the autumn.

Prophetically, it speaks of the time when God will again dwell with His people. John 1:14 says: "And the Word became flesh and dwelt (tabernacled) among us, and we beheld His glory, the glory as of the only begotten of the Father, full of grace and truth."

When King Solomon finished building the Temple, he dedicated it on the Feast of Tabernacles. 2 Chronicles 5:1 says, "So all the work that Solomon had done for the house of the Lord was finished; and Solomon brought in the things that his father David had dedicated: the silver and the gold and all the furnishings. And he put them in the treasuries of the house of God.

"Now Solomon assembled the elders of Israel and all the heads of the tribes, the chief fathers of the children of Israel, in Jerusalem, that they might bring the ark of the covenant of the Lord up from the City of David, which is Zion. Therefore all the men of Israel assembled with the king at the feast, which was in the seventh month. Then they brought up the ark, the tabernacle of meeting, and all the holy furnishings that were in the tabernacle..."

Then there followed many sacrifices of animals. 2 Chronicles 5:7 says, "Then the priests brought in the ark of the covenant of the Lord to its place in the inner sanctuary of the temple, to the Most Holy Place, under the wings of the cherubim...

2 Chronicles 5:13 "indeed it came to pass, when the trumpeters and singers were as one, to make one sound to be heard in praising and thanking the Lord, and when they lifted up their voice with the trumpets and cymbals and instruments of music, and praised the Lord, saying: 'For He is good and His mercy endures forever' – that the house, the house of the Lord, was filled with a cloud, so the priests could not continue

ministering because of the cloud; for the glory of the Lord filled the house of God."

Then Solomon prayed a long prayer, with supplications to the Lord, as recorded in 2 Chronicles 6.

2 Chronicles 7:1 "When Solomon had finished praying, fire came down from heaven and consumed the burnt offering and the sacrifices, and THE GLORY OF THE LORD FILLED THE TEMPLE. And the priests could not enter the house of the Lord, because the glory of the Lord had filled the Lord's house.

There was a great celebration as the magnificent temple was dedicated to the Lord.

Some believe that Jesus was actually born then:

1. Because of the verse just mentioned, in John 1:14.

2. Because the fall was the time when shepherds were more likely to be out in the fields with their sheep at night.

3. It is possible to determine when John the Baptist was conceived. See Luke 1:5. That says that John's father, the priest Zacharias, was of the division of Abijah. His division served during June-July. That was when the angel Gabriel announced to him that his wife would conceive and bear a son. (Luke 1:13-17). When the angel announced to Mary that she would conceive and bear a Son (Luke 1:31), he told her that John the Baptist was already six months along (Luke 1:36). That would mean that John would be born December-January. That would put the birth of Jesus in September-October.

(Perry Stone, "The Meal That Heals.")

Chapter Fourteen

THE FEAST OF TABERNACLES
(continued)

John 7:37: "On the last day, that great day of the feast, Jesus stood and cried out, saying, "If anyone thirsts, let them come to Me and drink. They who believe in Me, as the

Scripture has said, out of their innermost being will flow rivers of living water." But He spoke this concerning the Holy Spirit, whom those believing in Him would receive; for the Holy Spirit was not yet given, because Jesus was not yet glorified.

On the last day of the Feast of Tabernacles, the High Priest carried a jar of water from the Pool of Siloam, accompanied by a large procession, and poured the water out at the temple. This is what happened then. The pouring of the water signified the prayers of the people – for rain and for the Holy Spirit to be poured out on His people. Jesus stood up and announced Himself as the answer to that prayer!

He was the living water AND the giver of the Holy Spirit!

"Siloam" means "sent." John 9:7. There are over thirty times in the book of John when Jesus referred to Himself as the One the Father "sent"!

Jesus is the living water the people were praying for!

HARVEST OF SOULS: This harvest is mentioned in Revelation 14:14-16: "Then I looked, and behold, a white cloud, and on the cloud sat One like the Son of Man, having on His head a golden crown, and in His hand a sharp sickle. And another angel came out of the temple, crying with a loud voice to Him who sat on the cloud, "Thrust in Your sickle and reap, for the time has come for You to reap, for the harvest of the earth is ripe." So He who sat on the cloud thrust in His sickle on the earth, and the earth was reaped."

The first harvest (those who are saved?)

Now heed what Jesus tells His disciples in Matthew 13:37-45: "He who sows the good seed is the Son of man, the tares (weeds) are the people of the wicked one. The enemy who sowed them is the devil, the harvest is the end of the age and the reapers are the angels. Therefore, as the tares are gathered and burned in the fire, so it will be at the end of this age. The Son of man will send out His angels, and they will gather out of His kingdom all things that offend and those who practice lawlessness, and will cast them into the furnace of fire. There will be wailing and gnashing of teeth. Then the righteous will shine forth as the sun in the kingdom of their Father. They who have ears, let them hear!"

In Leviticus 23:33-34, Moses tells the people God's instructions for the celebration:

Leviticus 23:39 – they were to celebrate after they had gathered in the crops - the final celebration of the year!

So the Church of Jesus Christ is looking forward to when the final ingathering of the Church will take place – when all those to come to Christ will have come!

This will be a time of GREAT CELEBRATION! Remember it will be a time of "whoever will…." Revelation 22:16-17….a harvest of souls as never before!

Revelation 21:3 – And I heard a loud voice from heaven saying, "Behold, the tabernacle of God is with people, and He will dwell with them, and they shall be His people. God Himself will be with them and be their God. And God will wipe away every tear from their eyes; there shall be no more death, nor sorrow, nor crying. There shall be no more pain, for the former things have passed away."

Revelation 22:17: And the Spirit and the bride say, "Come!" And let them who hear say, "Come!" And let them who thirst come. Whoever desires, let them take the water of life freely.

Are YOU ready? Do you want to be a part of His great harvest of souls?

Are you willing to give yourself to Him in repentance and faith?

Are you ready to reach out your hands to Him and say, "Come, Lord Jesus!?"

If you have never prayed a prayer of salvation, you can say something like this:

Lord Jesus, I invite You to come in and take over my life. I believe that You are the Son of God, and that You died so that I might be forgiven and have eternal life. I am sorry for my sins. Please help me to follow You. Thank You, Lord. Amen.

AMEN!!

Afterword

Definition of "Afterword": Typically about the book's subject. It is used to supply extra material not covered in the main part of the book.

The symbolism of the feasts is similar to that of the Wilderness Tabernacle and its furnishings. The Passover in Egypt corresponds to the bronze altar where sacrifices were offered as atonement for sin. Israel's passage through the Red Sea after leaving Egypt corresponds to the bronze laver (water basin) in the Tabernacle.

The third feast, Firstfruits, was for the purpose of offering to God the first of their crops after their arrival in the Promised Land.

So God gave them Manna, His bread from heaven, to sustain them on their journey.

The fourth feast was Pentecost, the Law of God, written on two tablets of stone – in other words, the Ten Commandments.

The fifth feast was the Blowing of Trumpets.

The sixth feast, the Day of Atonement, was when all Israel confessed their sins and went before the High Priest as he performed the ceremonies for that great day.

The seventh and last festival was called the Feast of Tabernacles, or Ingathering, or Booths.

There could be no ingathering of crops as they made their way through the desert, but the name "The Feast of Booths" would take on real significance.

The Wilderness Tabernacle

After Israel left Egypt and after they had gone through the Red Sea, God called Moses up to the top of Mt. Sinai, where Moses spent 40 days and 40 nights alone with God, while the people waited below in their tents.

While there, God gave him instructions on how they should worship Him. They were not to go to a high rock, or some high hill, or a leafy tree, as idolaters did in the days of Noah and in the days of Sodom and Gomorrah. That is why the Lord wiped them out. No, the people of God were to worship Him in HIS way, and in the place HE would choose. These are the instructions God gave to Moses:

Exodus 25: "Take an offering from the people (of precious metals and stones…) and let them make Me a sanctuary, that I MAY DWELL AMONG THEM."

God's instructions to Moses, just before leaving Egypt, Exodus 12:35: "Now the children of Israel had done according to the word of Moses, and they had asked of the Egyptians articles of silver, articles of gold, and clothing. And the Lord had given the people favor in the sight of the Egyptians, so they granted them what they requested. Thus they plundered the Egyptians."

So the people of Israel were then able to give the offering that God commanded in Exodus 25:1-8.

As you read Exodus 25, you can see that God wanted His people to do things *His* way, not their own way, like the other nations did. Doing things God's way is what brings peace and satisfaction. God is a God who is near and not far off.

The Ark of The Covenant

The first article, and the most important, was the ARK, the place

God planned to dwell in their midst. What a concept! The mighty and everlasting God, the God who made the earth and the skies and the seas, with all their vastness – wants to dwell in intimate closeness to His people! To you and me!!

Exodus 25:10 – the Ark was to be made of acacia wood (a very durable wood, and plentiful). Then it was to be overlaid with gold, which was symbolic of deity, "inside and out." Verse 11. He also instructed them to make two poles, for the purpose of transporting the Ark as they moved from place to place during their journey through the wilderness on their way to the Promised Land.

The Ark was to contain the testimony which God gave them – the Ten Commandments (Exodus 20).

In Exodus 25:17, God tells Moses to make a Mercy Seat with cherubim (angels) looking toward the Ark and guarding it. God tells Moses He will speak to His people from the Mercy Seat. What mercy, grace, condescension, and love God demonstrates toward His people!

There are three classes of angels mentioned in the Bible - cherubim, seraphim, and archangels. One archangel is so called in the Bible: Michael (Jude 1:9). The angel Gabriel appeared to Mary to announce the birth of Jesus, as well as to Zacharias the priest, to announce the birth of John the Baptist. The Bible does not say that he is an archangel, although he may be. He also appeared to Daniel after Daniel had been praying and fasting - Daniel 8:16.

The name of the angel who rebelled against God and became the devil, or Satan, is Lucifer. He is called a "cherub" in Ezekiel 28:11-19. "Cherub" is the singular form of "cherubim." Lucifer is also referred to in Isaiah 14:12-15, by his name.

Cherubim are also mentioned in Ezekiel 10. When Adam and Eve sinned and God cast them out of the Garden of Eden, He placed cherubim outside the garden to keep anyone from entering.

Cherubim seem to function as guardians.

Seraphim are mentioned in Isaiah 6:2, at the time of Isaiah's calling to be a prophet.

THE TABLE OF SHOWBREAD

The next article was the Table (Exodus 25:23-30). This was for the bread, called the showbread, which the priests would eat as part of their ceremony (Leviticus 24:5-9).

Jesus said, "I am the Bread of Life. They who come to Me shall never hunger, and

they who believe in Me shall never thirst."
(John 6:35)

THE LAMPSTAND

Next was the Lampstand (Exodus 25:31-40). It was for the purpose of giving light to the priests as they ministered inside the Tabernacle. How important is light? During the plague of darkness in Egypt the Israelites were the only ones who had light in their dwellings. David prayed, "Give light to my eyes, or I will sleep in the shadow of death." Psalm 13:3 (NIV)

Most people would agree that eyesight would be the most difficult sense to do without.

Jesus said, "I am the Light of the world. They who follow Me shall not walk in darkness but shall have the light of life." (John 8:12)

THE TENT

Exodus 26:1-14: God gives Moses specific instructions for the construction of the tent (Tabernacle) itself. It was to be made of fine linen woven with blue, purple and scarlet threads. Note the symbolism of the colors: Blue (heavenly), purple (royalty), and red (blood).

THE COVERINGS

Exodus 26:14: God gives instructions for the coverings for the Tabernacle – ram skins dyed red with a covering of badger skins over the ram skins, to protect it from the elements.

THE FRAME

Exodus 26:15: Instructions for the frame of the Tabernacle, or tent. The boards were to be made of the durable acacia wood. They were to stand on foundation sockets of silver (verses 19-25).

Exodus 26:30: Bars of acacia wood were to be made to fortify the structure of the tent, and they were to be overlaid with gold.

THE INNER VEIL

Exodus 26:31: The Inner Veil. This was to shield the Ark from the view of anyone except the High Priest, who was commanded by God to enter the Most Holy Place on the Day of Atonement, and that only once a year. If anyone else presumed to go behind the Veil, they would die.

Note the sad story of Nadab and Abihu, Aaron's two older sons. They presumptuously dared to perform services to God in His sanctuary in a way God did not command. They were immediately struck down and burned with fire because of their presumption and irreverence. Leviticus 10:2 says, "So fire went out from the Lord and devoured them, and they died before the Lord."

THE DOOR (OUTER VEIL)

The next article was the Door (Exodus 26:36), also called the Outer Veil, or the Screen. It was constructed very much like the Inner Veil, except without the interwoven design of cherubim. Both veils were very beautiful, as was the inside of the Tabernacle itself. The Door was as far as a common person (non-priest) could go when he offered his sacrifice.

Then Jesus said to them again, "Most assuredly I say to you, I am the Door of the sheep."

THE COURT

Exodus 27:9 – The Court of the Tabernacle: It was made of white curtains, or hangings, which surrounded the Tabernacle, keeping others besides Israelites out. They were set on socket foundations of bronze. The bands, or rods for the curtains, were made of silver.

THE GATE

Exodus 27:16 - On the east side of the Court was the Gate, through which the people entered to bring their offerings. The Gate was to be made of fine linen, interwoven with blue, purple and scarlet. No one but Israelites were permitted to go through the Gate.

THE OIL FOR THE LAMPSTAND

Exodus 27:20-21. Instructions for the Oil to light the Lampstand: It was to be made of pure oil of pressed olives and was for the purpose of keeping the lamps continually burning, never to go out. See Matthew 25:1-13, where Jesus tells the story of the wise and foolish virgins, or bridesmaids, who were waiting for the Bridegroom. The foolish virgins allowed their lamps to go out and were shut out of the wedding celebration.

Luke 12:35 says, "Let your waist be girded and your lamps burning."

THE ALTAR OF INCENSE

Exodus 30:1-7. The Altar of Incense was to be placed in front of the Inner Veil. It was to be made of acacia wood overlaid with gold. The High Priest was to burn incense on it every morning and every evening at twilight when he lit the lamps before the Lord.

Exodus 30:34-38.The incense for the altar was made of sweet spices and beaten very fine. None were permitted to make any for themselves.

The Lord loves good smells! And so do we. We hope to be a "sweet smelling fragrance to the Lord." 2 Corinthians 2:15. Also see Philippians 4:18, where Paul refers to the gift sent by the church at Philippi as a "sweet-smelling aroma, an acceptable sacrifice, well pleasing to God."

Exodus 30:17. The Laver, or wash basin, was to be made of bronze. It was for the priests to wash their hands and feet before they went into the Tabernacle, and after they came out.

Everything about the Tabernacle was portable – the tent itself as well as the furnishings, since they would be taking it all along with them on their journey through the wilderness. See Hebrews 13:14, which says, "Here we have no continuing city, but we seek one to come." In other words, Christians are not supposed to settle down in this world, since we look forward to a better place to come. Paul called the

Ephesians "strangers and foreigners" before they came to Christ. Ephesians 2:19.

Numbers 3 and 4 set forth the duties of the Levites for the taking down, the transporting, and the setting up of the Tabernacle.

Similarities between the Feasts and the Tabernacle:

> Passover and Bronze Altar: Sacrifice for sins.

> Laver and Unleavened Bread: Cleansing and separation from their enemies as Israel crossed the Red Sea.

Sheaf of Firstfruits: Feast to be celebrated after Israel was in the Promised Land. In the meantime, the Lord sustained them with the miraculous bread from heaven, called "manna." He commanded Moses to store some in a pot and keep it in the Most

Holy Place, before the Ark – to remind them of how God took care of them during those forty years of wilderness wanderings. Exodus 16:32-35.

The Feast of Pentecost: Moses went up Mount Sinai, after God had called him up to Him - Exodus 19. He received the Ten Commandments, written on two tablets of stone, "by the finger of God." Exodus 31:18.

God commanded Moses to put the testimony which He gave him into the Ark. Exodus 25:16

The Feast of Pentecost was to be celebrated every year – with two loaves of bread made WITH yeast.

In Matthew 13:33, Jesus illustrates the growth of the Kingdom of God by comparing it to yeast, which a woman bakes into bread. "The kingdom of heaven is like leaven, which a woman took and hid in three measures of meal till it was all leavened." Here we see leaven used in a positive sense.

The festival was to be celebrated fifty days (or seven weeks) after the waving of the Sheaf of Firstfruits. See Leviticus 23:15-22.

The Feast of the Blowing of Trumpets: Celebrated by Israel on the first day of the New Year (Rosh Hashanah). Trumpets were blown, as well as the ram's horn (shofar). It ushered in the "Ten Days of Awe," before the Day of Atonement. Psalm 81:3.

Trumpets throughout the Bible signify the voice of God speaking to His people: Revelation 1:10; Exodus 19:16, 19, 20; 1 Thessalonians 4:16.

Numbers 10:1-7. And the Lord spoke to Moses, saying, "Make two silver trumpets… use them for calling the congregation and for directing the movement of the camps. When they blow both of them, all the congregation shall gather before you at the door of the Tabernacle of meeting. But if they blow only one, then the leaders, the heads of the divisions of Israel, shall gather to you. When you sound the advance the camps that lie on the east side shall begin their journey. When you sound the advance the second time, then the camps that lie on the south side shall begin their journey…."

And when the assembly is to be gathered together, you shall blow, but not sound the advance. The sons of Aaron the priest shall blow the trumpets; and these shall be to you as an ordinance forever throughout your generations." Numbers 10:9.

There was a short trumpet blast, and a longer one, called the "advance."

Numbers 10:9: "When you go to war in your land against the enemy who oppresses you, then you shall sound an alarm with the trumpets, and you will be remembered before the Lord your God, and you will be saved from your enemies."

Numbers 10:10: "Also in the day of your gladness, in your appointed feasts and at the beginning of your months, you shall blow the trumpets over your burnt offerings and over the sacrifices of your peace offerings, and they shall be a memorial for you before your God."

Israel became a fighting force in the wilderness. There were battles to be fought as they traveled. See Exodus 17, where Amalek waylaid them as they came out of Egypt. God announced, "The Lord will have war with Amalek from generation to generation." (Verse 14)

In Numbers 1, God ordered them to take a census of all the fighting men from age 20 years and above – "all who are able to go to war in Israel." (Verse 3)

The two silver trumpets would be used extensively as they marched, as well as when they were in their promised land and needed to establish their residence there.

God ordered a second census after the Israelites had been in the wilderness forty years and would soon be entering their promised land (Numbers 26:2). At that time all the people who started on their trek had died because of their refusal to believe that they could overcome their enemies (See Numbers 13:1-25). Only Joshua and Caleb would be permitted to enter because they believed God's promise.

The Day of Atonement:

The High Priest entered the Most Holy Place before the Ark of the Covenant, as God ordered him to do on this most holy day, to make atonement for the sins of the people.

The Mercy Seat inside the Inner Veil:

This was the most beautiful room in the Tabernacle. It was all gold. The ceiling was also beautiful, made of fine linen woven with blue, purple and scarlet threads, with artistic designs of cherubim woven in. Exodus 26:1. The High Priest was permitted to enter only once a year, and only he was permitted to enter.

The High Priest's garments were also very beautiful. See Exodus 28:2 – "And you shall make holy garments for Aaron your brother FOR GLORY AND FOR BEAUTY."

Does God love beauty? Just look at the world around us – the trees, flowers, grasses, skies, glorious sunsets, beautiful seas, rivers, brooks, twinkling stars in the night sky…! And what is more beautiful than a rainbow?!

And we have the most beautiful High Priest of all – the Lord Jesus Christ!

> The Feast of Tabernacles, also called the Feast of Ingathering, Harvest and Booths.

As the Tabernacle made its way through the wilderness, we see the significance of the name "Booths." There would be no harvesting or ingathering while in the wilderness. But the name "Booths" was very applicable. It was how God provided comfort and protection for His people through the hot days and cold nights in the desert. Over the tent would be a cloud to cool them off during the day, and a pillar of fire to keep them warm at night.

So God commanded when they kept the Feast of Tabernacles, or Booths, as part of the celebration long afterwards, to construct little shelters of leafy boughs to dwell in during the seven days of the festival. See Nehemiah 8:1-18. Verse 14 – "And they found written in the Law, which the Lord had commanded by Moses, that the children of Israel should dwell in booths during the Feast of the seventh month, and they should announce and proclaim in all their cities and in Jerusalem, saying, "Go out to the mountains and bring olive branches, myrtle branches, palm branches, and branches of leafy trees, to make booths, as it is written."

"Then the people went out and brought them, and made themselves booths, each one on the roof of his house, or in their courtyards, or the courts of the house of God, and in the open square of the Water Gate and in the open square of the Gate of Ephraim. So the whole assembly...made booths and sat under them...And there was very great gladness."

Nehemiah 8:18 says that they kept the feast seven days. He goes on to say, "Also day by day, from the first day until the last day, he read from the book of the Law of God."

There is also a personal aspect to the Feasts:

We keep the Feast of Passover when we are born again – when we accept the blood of Jesus Christ as our sacrifice for sins.

We keep the Feast of Unleavened Bread when we are water baptized.

We keep the Feast of the Sheaf of Firstfruits when we give offerings to God for His blessings to us.

We keep the Feast of Pentecost when we are baptized in the Holy Spirit.

We keep the Feast of Trumpets when we evangelize and tell the Good News to whomever!

We look forward to the Day of Atonement, when our Lord appears to take us home, as 1 Thessalonians 4:16 says, "For the Lord Himself will descend from heaven with a shout, with the voice of an archangel, and with the trumpet of God. And the dead in Christ will rise first. Then we who are alive and remain shall be caught up with them in the clouds to meet the Lord in the air. So shall we ever be with the Lord."

And we can keep the Feast of Harvest, or Ingathering, when we share the gospel, when we support missionaries, or become a missionary ourselves, to spread the Good News of Jesus throughout the world. And we can celebrate the harvest of souls won to the Lord daily through the work of missionaries – and ordinary people like you and me!

Epilogue

I would like to conclude this book by sharing how the feasts of the Lord are being fulfilled in my own life.

I was born in 1934 to parents who were good people – but they had no interest in God or church or religion.

During the first five years of my life I don't remember that thoughts about God ever crossed my mind.

When I was about five, I was playing with my little friend next door. She went to the Catholic Church and wanted to play like we were going to confession. She told me what they did – and I remember thinking that I wouldn't really like to do that – but I played along.

Soon after I asked my mother what happens to people when they die. She replied, "If they are good, they go to heaven, and if they are bad, they go to hell."

So I asked her more about heaven and hell, and she told me what she remembered as a girl when they went to church occasionally.

This concerned me. I wanted to be sure I would go to heaven when I died.

I went to church three or four times with my friend. I was very impressed when she made her first communion, along with others her age. The little girls all looked so beautiful in their white dresses.

I wanted to continue going to church – but didn't particularly want to go to the

Catholic Church because I didn't like the part about confessing my sins to someone else. Not that I was a great sinner at five or six years of age, but....

So my mother found someone else to take me to a Methodist Sunday School. I liked that, and even went with them on a picnic one day.

When I was about eight, my father was transferred to a small town called Barstow, in the Mojave Desert. I wanted to go to Sunday School, so my mother found someone to take me to the local Congregational Church.

I enjoyed going to that Sunday School, and was able to walk there by myself. I won a nice white Bible for memorizing all the books of the Bible. I was so proud of that Bible! It was the first one I ever had.

When we moved to another town, Richmond, I was in junior high, and found a Presbyterian church I could walk to. I got my girlfriend Hilda to go with me. That was good, but my dad got transferred a year later to Fresno, which was too big a city for me to walk to church – and where would I go?

So, I didn't go to Sunday School for a while.

Then we got some new neighbors who moved in next door, with whom my parents became good friends. They attended a denominational church. I pestered my mom to take me. I especially wanted to be baptized. The day finally came!

We all went to church about twenty miles away. Finally came the day I was longing for – they were going to have a baptism! My father, sister and brother and I were all baptized, by sprinkling, in front of the church. It was a momentous time for me! I cried because I felt I was pleasing God. My mother didn't join in because she had been baptized as a girl.

I was about 14, and we started going regularly, and I met the other young people, including the pastor's daughter Carolyn, who was a year older than I. Also another girl, Kay, became one of my best friends.

I became a Sunday School teacher and also joined the youth group. I was happy with my experience.

When I got my driver's license at 16, I began to go mostly by myself. Sometimes my best friend Jeane would go with me.

When I left for college at the University of California in Berkeley, I stopped being interested in church. I was more interested in my social life. But when my husband and I were married in 1956, I began to think about God again. After we moved to San Jose, California, and while we were expecting our first child, we went to a church we found of the denomination I had gone to in Fresno. In fact, the first time we went I began to have labor pains!

We stopped going for a while. One day, the pastor of that church came to visit me. He admired our beautiful little girl and asked us to come back. We did, and spent eleven years in that church.

We became active and became leaders of the youth group, a ministry which we both enjoyed immensely.

But one thing bothered me...how do I know that I am pleasing God? Do I have enough faith to go to heaven?

One day, years later, after our fourth child was born, a couple of the same denomination came to our Sunday School class for the purpose of presenting to us the little booklet called "The Four Spiritual Laws." They talked about being "born again" – something we weren't taught.

When we went back home, I went through the booklet by myself. I prayed the suggested prayer but didn't feel any real assurance.

I asked a friend in our church how we get born again. She answered, "I guess when you're baptized." OK, so that would mean babies are born again through their parents' getting them baptized.

Our Bible study group all agreed that children were definitely sinners and yes, indeed, they needed to be baptized.

But I still wasn't satisfied. There still seemed to be an emptiness inside me.

One day I fell to my knees in desperation, confessing to God my inability to be what

He wanted me to be, and He would have to do the work in me Himself.

That is what He was waiting for! My burden was lifted – I felt joyful and light-hearted.

The amazing thing was the singing of my heart! I had never heard of such a thing. And the enormous love I felt for the Lord! And the way I began loving the Bible! I had my regular morning devotions, but they were mostly just exercises that I went through to "do my duty and please God."

I wonder if any of you have had that same feeling of just "going through the motions"?

Anyway, my life was totally changed. I tried to share my experience with our Bible study group, but they were resistant and didn't agree.

My husband didn't agree with me either, and we had some stressful times. He asked me if

I loved Jesus more than him, and I truthfully answered "yes." We even discussed divorce. I said I didn't want a divorce, but I wasn't going to put him ahead of Jesus.

There is a verse in 1 Peter 3:1, which became a true guide for me at that time: "Wives, likewise, be submissive to your own husbands, that even if some do not obey the word, they, without a word, may be won by the conduct of their wives, when they observe your chaste conduct..." In other words, I should keep my mouth shut!

On Christmas of that year, 1968, we went to church. My husband took a moment to pray his own prayer as the pastor was praying the liturgy: "Lord, if she's right, please let me know!"

He said immediately it felt as if a huge weight had suddenly lifted off him. He began to feel light and joyful!

After the service he told me about it. I could hardly believe it – I was so happy! That Christmas was the best ever!

We found a different church. Our friends in our Bible study group began to feel uncomfortable with us. In fact, they finally didn't even tell us where the next meetings would be held. This made us sad that we would lose all the friends we had during those eleven years.

However, our new church was such a wonderful experience! It was just what I was looking for.

So in January of 1969 my husband Norman and I were both baptized by "dunking"! Those were truly glory days!

So now I had experienced the first two feasts – Passover and real salvation as the blood of Christ washed away my sins. I knew He had done it before, since I had prayed a lot for it, but now it was a real experience for me. That happened on Memorial Day, 1968.

My husband's experience happened on Christmas, 1968. So in January, 1969, we experienced the second feast, Unleavened Bread, as we were water baptized.

On December 2, 1968, I received the ability to pray in other tongues when my friend and teacher, Anna, prayed for me at my kitchen table. It was glorious!

In our new church Norman began to seek the Holy Spirit with the ability to speak in tongues. Six men from our new church went forward to the altar every Sunday evening to receive prayer for the Baptism in the Holy Spirit.

It was in May on Memorial Day, 1969, that Norm finally received! He was so elated! He couldn't stop speaking in tongues during the 30-minute drive home!

Our two older children, Diana and Matthew, witnessed what happened to their father. They decided they wanted it too! Diana was eleven and Matt was almost eight.

So they went to the altar for prayer the next Sunday night. It wasn't long before they were each speaking in tongues!

They always bickered a lot, as most brothers and sisters do. But after their experience of being filled with the Holy Spirit, they were loving and sweet to each other for about three days! It was wonderful!

So that is how the feasts of Passover, Unleavened Bread, and Pentecost, were fulfilled in my life, my husband's life, and the lives of our two older children.

The Lord let me know that the "Sheaf of Firstfruits" (Feast #3), would be the first believer we win to the Lord. My friend Palma became my Sheaf of Firstfruits when I got her to come to my kitchen table Bible study. I knew Palma well from our former church. She was a great helper in our youth group and helped with cooking and serving meals at our youth retreats. I told her my story of how the Lord had come to me. That stirred up a desire in Palma for the same experience. Anna prayed for her to receive Jesus as her Savior. Palma started to come to our new church and fully entered in to the praise, worship, activities and ministry of the church. She spent many years there. She was one of my best friends – she is now with the Lord in heaven.

Seven or eight months after we started attending our new church, a presbytery of three elders from other churches came to pray for those candidates who had fasted and prayed and wanted to receive the "Laying on of Hands" in order to find God's direction for their lives and how He wanted to use them. This would have been the fifth feast I discussed in my section on the seven feasts.

It was held for three or four evenings – however long it took to minister to all the candidates. As I recall, it took at least three evenings, maybe more.

I remember my husband Norman was told that he was a "Pillar" in the church. Remember that these ministers weren't from our church and didn't know anything about the people they were ministering to. Norm was such a pillar in our churches, both in San Jose and in our present church in Mariposa! A pillar is strong and supports the building. It is something you can lean upon! That was definitely my husband.

He was also told he would teach. He did teach a lot – in Bible College as well as in our churches. He was a good teacher – not only in my opinion, but also in the opinion of those who listened to him.

One of the presbyters said he would have faith for finances. He served for years as business administrator in our church, while I was the church bookkeeper. He had a keen business sense, which our pastors appreciated.

I was told that I was a mediator – in other words, an intercessor in prayer. That has definitely taken place in the fifty years since! I have had many instances of heavy weeping and crying out to God for people I barely knew or didn't know at all. I remember that while we were still in our first church in San Jose (after I knew I was born again), that I heard about the husband of one of the women in our church at that time who had an accident at work and his arm was cut off. I didn't know the man, and barely knew the wife, but I began to weep and cry out to God for him for at least half an hour.

Once I got a phone call from a woman in our church, informing me that a church member was driving on the highway and had a horrible accident, in which her only son (about nine) was killed. That affected me deeply. I lay on the floor and wept and cried for that family for at least an hour. Unfortunately my intercession didn't bring the boy back to life, but God did use it for good in the family's lives. The mother and girls all recovered and went on to serve the Lord. Two of the girls married young men in our church.

Another time of heavy intercession was when there was a huge wildfire in Oakhurst, the town south of us. I lay on my bed for an hour and wept and prayed for the fire to miss the huge propane tank northeast of town. I also prayed for all the businesses in Oakhurst and all my friends there. There were no homes or businesses destroyed, and the fire curved around the propane tank as it continued northeast of town. I imagine that there were other intercessors praying as well, but it was so gratifying to me to be a part.

When we had a wildfire near our own area in Mariposa and had to be evacuated, I didn't feel the heavy need to pray in the same way as I had before.

My granddaughter Lindsey has a friend that I began to have a heavy burden of prayer for. I don't know why...I loved her like I loved my granddaughter's other friends, but for this one I felt a special concern. I was especially concerned about her finishing school. When she dropped out, I wept and prayed and cried out to God for her for a long time. I remember feeling so very grieved. However, she has become at her still young age a very successful woman in her business. God has blessed her in many ways. Sometimes I don't understand why I have felt such a need to pray and travail, but God knows and uses it for His good purposes.

The Bible says, "Likewise, the Spirit also helps in our weaknesses. For we do not know what we should pray for as we ought, but the Spirit Himself makes intercession for us with groanings which cannot be uttered. Now He who searches the hearts knows what the mind of the Spirit is, because He makes intercession for the saints according to the will of God." Romans 8:26-27.

I was also told that I had a ministry of showing mercy. That has proven to be true as well. At one time Norm and I were driving by a fast foods restaurant. He saw a woman crying on the side of the parking lot. He stopped while I went over to her and asked if I could pray for her. She accepted my prayer and seemed grateful.

There were a number of people in our churches who weren't able to drive to church. Picking them up and taking them to church was something we did quite regularly. My daughter remembers that we did that. She remembers having to sit in the back seat with some of them "who didn't smell very good."

There was a young woman with a newborn attending our church, whose stepson shot and killed his father, her husband. She needed another place to stay, so she stayed with us for about a couple of weeks. Her baby girl was one day older than our baby girl.

We became good friends. One day, to show her appreciation, she fixed a Korean barbecue for us. That was one of the most delicious meals I have ever had! I became a great fan of Kim-Chee!

I had an older friend, Edna, who needed a temporary place to stay. She moved in with us for a few weeks. She was a Type 1 diabetic and required insulin shots every day. Since she was nearly blind, she wasn't able to give herself shots any more. So I had to learn how. I practiced on an orange. She warned me against an air bubble getting into the syringe – lest it kill her! As you can imagine, that made me very nervous, but I managed to do it successfully (with much prayer!) After a few weeks she moved in with her sister.

Another time my husband and I drove all the way to Turlock, about 100 miles away, to pick up a woman in our church who had just had surgery.

My daughter Sara has a very strong gift of mercy. She and I together have reached out to a number of women in our mountain area.

I was told that I would prophesy. I was happy to receive that gift, but it was also kind of scary! What if I said something that was not from God, but just my own idea? I guess everyone goes through that. But I got so I could prophesy fairly confidently after a while. Once I started to prophesy and shortly after I just stopped – couldn't say another word. I felt foolish, but immediately one of our elders on the platform finished it for me. That was a relief!

There was a couple in our church who were going through a rough patch in their marriage. In fact, the wife wasn't sure she wanted to go on with it.

We were attending our small group meeting when a verse from 1 Peter 5:10 came strongly to me: "But may the God of all grace, who called us to His eternal glory by Christ Jesus, after you have suffered a while, perfect, establish, strengthen and settle you."

They moved away, but afterward we heard that things were going well for them. To God be the glory!

So that is my story of how the first five feasts have been fulfilled in my life and in my husband's.

Our wonderful Father in heaven wants to bless all people everywhere with the fullness of the feasts in their personal lives. I urge every believer to press into the fullness of what God has for YOU, personally. He wants all His children to experience the joy, satisfaction, excitement and fulfillment

He offers. Like any good father, He wants His children to experience abundant life!

Jesus says in John 10:10, "I have come that they may have life, and that more abundantly."

I have written my story as a testimony to the grace and wonder of our loving God. Even though I was a little girl with no religious background, He made sure that at least one in my family came to know Him. And from there He has made sure that my family members, whom I loved, have all made their way to heaven to be with Him.

I know of people with similar stories.

God is good and He loves all of us so passionately!

Appendix 1

The seven "I Am" Statements of Jesus:

John 6:35: "I am the Bread of Life. He who comes to Me shall never hunger, and he who believes in Me shall never thirst."

John 8:12: "I am the Light of the world. He who follows Me shall not walk in darkness, but have the light of life."

John 10:7: "I am the Door of the sheep. If anyone enters by Me, he will be saved, and will go in and out and find pasture."

John 10:14: "I am the good Shepherd. The good Shepherd gives His life for the sheep."

John 11:25: "I am the Resurrection and the Life. He who believes in Me, though he may die, he shall live. And whoever lives and believes in Me shall never die."

John 14:6: "I am the Way, the Truth and the Life. No one comes to the Father except through Me."

John 15:1-2: "I am the true Vine, and My Father is the Vinedresser. Every branch in Me that does not bear fruit He takes away; and every branch that bears fruit He prunes, that it may bear more fruit."

Appendix 2

BIBLE VERSES TO HELP US GO TO HEAVEN

John 3:16

Romans 3:23

Romans 5:3

Romans 5:8

Romans 6:23

Romans 10:13

Those left out of heaven:

Revelation 20:11-15

Revelation 21:8

Revelation 22:15

How to strengthen your faith: Read the Bible every day, for at least five minutes – preferably at a set time each day, when it is best for you. Some people prefer early morning, others just before bedtime. Busy mothers may want to read the Bible when their children are napping, or at school - whatever works for you. Just do it! Your faith and understanding will grow.

If you aren't used to Bible reading, start with the four gospels, and/or Psalms and Proverbs. It is also a good idea to get familiar with the Table of Contents. The books are mostly in chronological order.

I would also recommend the excellent little devotional book, "Jesus Calling," by Sarah Young. It is only two to three paragraphs long for each day. You will get to know Jesus better if you read it daily.

Appendix 3

GOD'S PLAN OF THE AGES

	First Dispensation		2,000 years
Gen. 3:1-7	Adam's Sin	4000 BC	
Gen. 5:24	Enoch Translated	3000 BC	
Gen. 6-9	Noah & the Flood	2500 BC	
Gen. 12-50	Abraham, Isaac, Jacob	2000 BC	
	Second Dispensation		2,000 years
Gen. 37-50	Joseph	2000 BC	
Ex. 1-40	Moses	1500 BC	
Num-Deut	The Exodus	1500 BC	
	The Kings	1000 BC	
	Kingdom Divided	500 BC	
	Jesus	0	
	Third Dispensation	2,000 years	
The Church Age	100 AD		
	The Popes	500 AD	
	The Dark Ages	1000 AD	
	Reformers (Luther, etc)	1500 AD	
	Second Coming	2000 AD	

Adapted from "God and His Word" by Ernest B. Gentile, who adapted his from Rev. W. H. Offiler

Appendix 4

SOME DIFFICULT QUESTIONS:

Disclaimer: I am not an authority, but I do have thoughts on some difficult questions in peoples' minds, which I am happy to share. I have done research on applicable Bible passages.

What is the unforgivable sin?

There are several verses in the Bible which carry a warning about a point beyond which one can go before salvation is no longer possible. They are Matthew 12:31-32; Hebrews 6:4-8; Hebrew 10:29.

I was concerned once that maybe I had committed the unforgivable sin – also called "The blasphemy against the Holy Spirit." I asked my pastor about it. His answer was that if I was concerned about, then I probably hadn't committed it. That is probably true.

Jesus warned the people that all kinds of sin against Him can be forgiven, but the blasphemy against the Holy Spirit can never be forgiven. Matthew 12:31-32.

I believe that is because it is the Holy Spirit who brings us the revelation of Jesus. To blaspheme Him would be rejecting the testimony He gives us about who Jesus is, and His redemptive work. When Jesus spoke these words, He was continually being spoken against and criticized. See Matthew 12:22-24

There will come a point when the Spirit no longer pursues them. The Bible says, "My Spirit will not strive with people forever." Genesis 6:3.

When Jesus was about to leave His disciples to go back to heaven, He assured them that He would not leave them alone, but that He would send them another Helper. Jesus is now back in heaven with the Father, but the Holy Spirit has come to earth to continue Jesus' work among people. The Holy Spirit is the only Person of the Holy Trinity who is on earth. When someone continually rejects His wooing, the Spirit will eventually leaves him/her alone. So that person chooses their own fate.

King Pharaoh of Egypt is an example of one who had gone beyond the point of forgiveness. Exodus 10:18, 27; 11:9-10; 11:20,27. He had changed his mind several times after telling Moses he would let the

Israelites go. Finally he had gone beyond the point of no return and forgiveness would no longer be granted. God said then to Moses, "Go in to Pharaoh; for I have hardened his heart and the hearts of his servants, that I may show these signs of mine before him..." Also in 10:20, God says He had hardened Pharaoh's heart.

Hebrews 6:4-8. Here again the person chooses their own fate. The ground was too hard (verse 8). Although the ground had been watered, the water did not sink in.

Hebrews 10:29 warns us of a believer who continues to sin and disobey God.

1. What about those who die without ever hearing the good news about Jesus taking our sins upon Himself and making the way for us to enter heaven?

Every human being is born with a conscience – an inner signal to let us know if we are doing something wrong. For instance, most nearly every culture knows that murder, stealing and lying are wrong. Also people in every culture know that kindness, respect for parents, and love for family are good. If a person truly lives according to their conscience, I don't believe God would punish them by sending them to hell – because they never had the chance to hear the Gospel.

There are other Bible teachers who believe this as well.

See Romans 2; Ezekiel 18.

There is also the story of Cornelius, a Roman centurion, who was a good man and spent his life blessing others and giving to charity. Acts 10. God told the Apostle Peter in a dream to go to him and preach the Gospel. The result was that Cornelius and his family, as well as his friends and neighbors, responded to the good news and became believers!

2. If a person dies without accepting Christ, even though family members had been praying for and witnessing to him/her for many years, is there any hope?

I would refer the reader to the best article I have ever read on that subject. It was written by Francis Frangipane and is entitled "The Silent Harvest."

3. Are there any children in hell? No. There is what is called "The age of accountability." Most Bible teachers say that is around twelve years of age.

Paul touches on this in Romans 7:9 and verses following.

I read a book once by a man who had gone to heaven for a while, before he returned to this life. He says that he was also taken into hell, as Jesus protected him in his arms. He related that he saw no children in hell.

Teenagers are subject to damnation and hell.

4. What does the Bible say about marriage?

My favorite verse on marriage is Ephesians 5:33 – "Nevertheless, let each one of you in particular so love his own wife as himself, and let the wife see that she respects her husband."

I read an exposition of that verse many years ago in an excellent book called "His Needs, Her Needs" by Willard F. Harley. He says that a woman's primary need is for love and security, and a man's primary need is for respect and admiration. Married couples need to remember that and render to their mate that which will most meet his/her needs.

Also see 1 Corinthians 7:3-5 for good advice for married couples.

Dedication

To my Lord and Savior Jesus Christ, who redeemed my life from the power of the grave and paid the price for my salvation:

Your love to me will always be

The only thing that meets my needs –

That lifts me up to heights unknown

Beyond the stars, unto Your throne.

In You I am forever blest –

In You alone I've found my rest,

My peace, my joy, my purpose too:

Loving, serving, praising You.

I also dedicate my book to my beloved husband, Norman, who graduated to heaven in January 2018.

Also to my four precious children: Diana, Matthew, John and Sara, whom I love with all my heart, as well as to their children, whom I also love with all my heart.

I also dedicate my book to my friends who have walked beside us for so many years, as well as my students, who have made teaching such a rewarding experience.

Bibliography

The Feasts of Israel and Their Spiritual Fulfillment (study sheets)	Ernest B. Gentile
The Temple: Its Ministries and Services	Alfred Edersheim
Unger's Bible Dictionary	Merrill F. Unger
The Feast of Passover	Ralph Mahoney
The Seventh Feast of the Seventh Month	John Robert Stevens
God, Gold and Glory "Fire on Azusa Street"	Henry Falany
God and His Word	Ernest B. Gentile
Why Apostles Now?	Ernest B. Gentile
Halley's Bible Handbook	Henry H. Halley
The Feast of Tabernacles	George H. Warnock
An Exposition of Leviticus	Andrew A. Bonar
The Path of the Just	B. Maureen Gagliardi

About the Author

I first taught on the Feasts of Israel when I taught classes in adult Sunday school, and later at Northern California Bible College. That was in San Jose, California. I enjoyed it immensely, and learned a lot through teaching. That is usually the way it is.

It was especially rewarding to see what I was teaching "strike a chord" with someone!

Through my teaching and taking classes at Bible College for several years, I was able to earn my Bachelor's Degree. I had earned my Associate's Degree while at the University of California in Berkeley years earlier.

My husband Norman and I were both ordained while in San Jose.

I wrote my first book, "Reflections," as a memorial and tribute to my husband, Norman, who left me for heaven in January of 2018.

We lived in San Jose, California, for the first forty years of our marriage. In 1997 we moved to Mariposa, California, where I presently live. My daughter Sara is my caregiver.